ACKNOWLEDGEMENTS

I have been lovingly supported by my wonderful
circle of friends including a rewarding
creative relationship with Aaron Chiffers.
They have helped me to develop this book and in doing so,
inspired me to share my artwork and my voice.

Thank you

PUBLISHED IN GREAT BRITAIN
2014
FIRST EDITION
LIMITED EDITION

This is copy number

30
―――
300

The Sea Garden is a painting that I loved creating.

It has been about my own journey of love, sharing wonderful, magical moments and opening such a richness of beauty in my heart for the man I loved. I discovered parts of myself that I did not know and enjoyed exploring each and every moment of them.

To love from the heart is a true gift and I give thanks for that, but sadly things change and it does not matter how true our intentions are we cannot control the outcomes of others.

This has been my own very personal journey out of my own sadness, grief, anger, despair, desire and love.

Writing this series of poems has been so very cathartic and healing for me. I truly feel that I have been through every emotion, which I have felt deeply, leaving me in a place I did not expect to be. What I am left with is a body of work that I have loved doing.

This is the voice that was never heard.

The Voice of The Sea Garden.

VOICE OF THE SEA GARDEN

When you found me I was not love

But in your eyes I saw God

The ocean rushed past me and I was cared for

A life a life I cried out loud I have found a life

Even in the deepest of water I felt safe

So I blossomed

Opening myself to the movement of you

I grew like a sea flower

Rich and delightful

Beautiful and magnificent

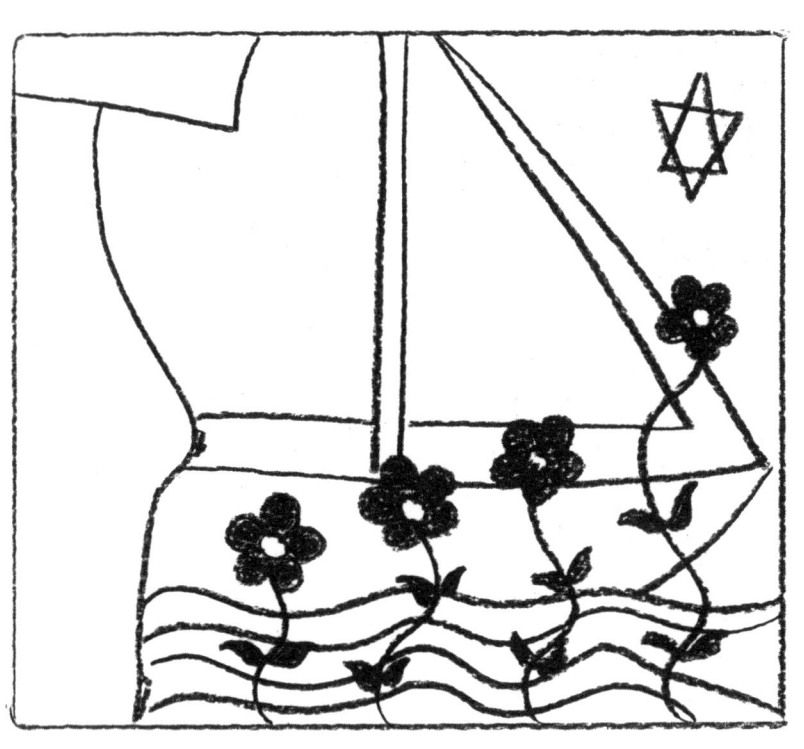

I spit out rage and rocks

Bile and pain

It comes to me like a storm

Howling vengeful

Dark are my thoughts

All is lost at sea

She pulls me under

I am swept to far shores

I am taken home

For my heart did not lose that love

The ocean shows me I am the sea flower

I can still spit rage and rocks

But I always come home

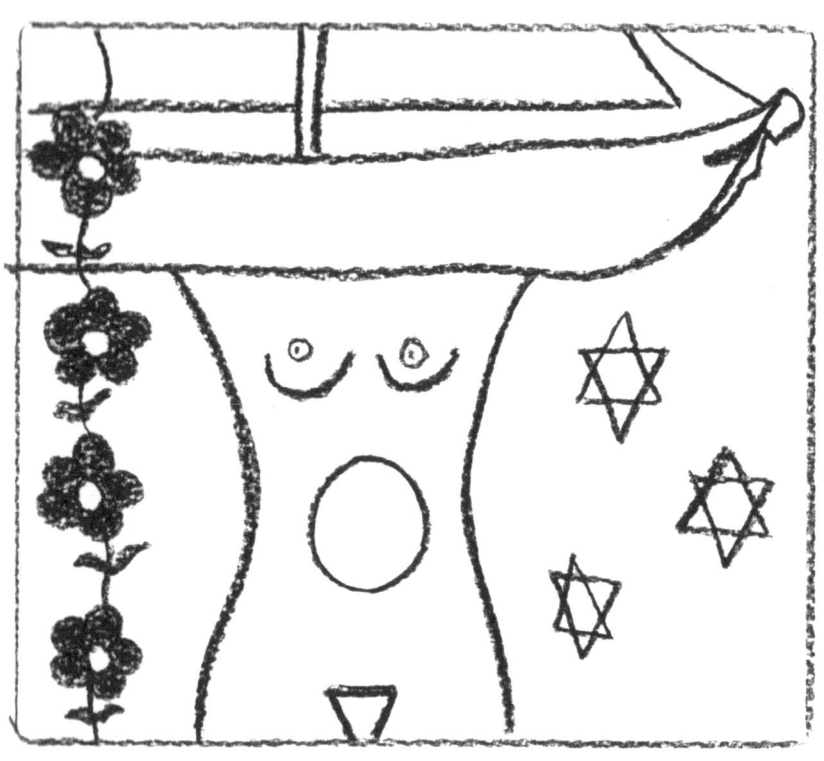

If I'd known it would have been the last time

A longer embrace I would have held onto

If I'd known it was the last time to feel your lips

The longest of kisses I would have held onto

If I'd known it was the last time

I would have not let you leave before we had made love

Or looked into your eyes and caressed your face

We never know it's going to be the last time

My sorrow my sorrow

I hold it like a wounded child

In my loving arms

I embrace you safely

While staring at starry skies

Some of the magic has been left for me

So into the ocean I must go

To wash my pain away

A blessed love a blessed man

I will find some peace the best I can

But you my love have you sorrow for me

Or just a broken heart

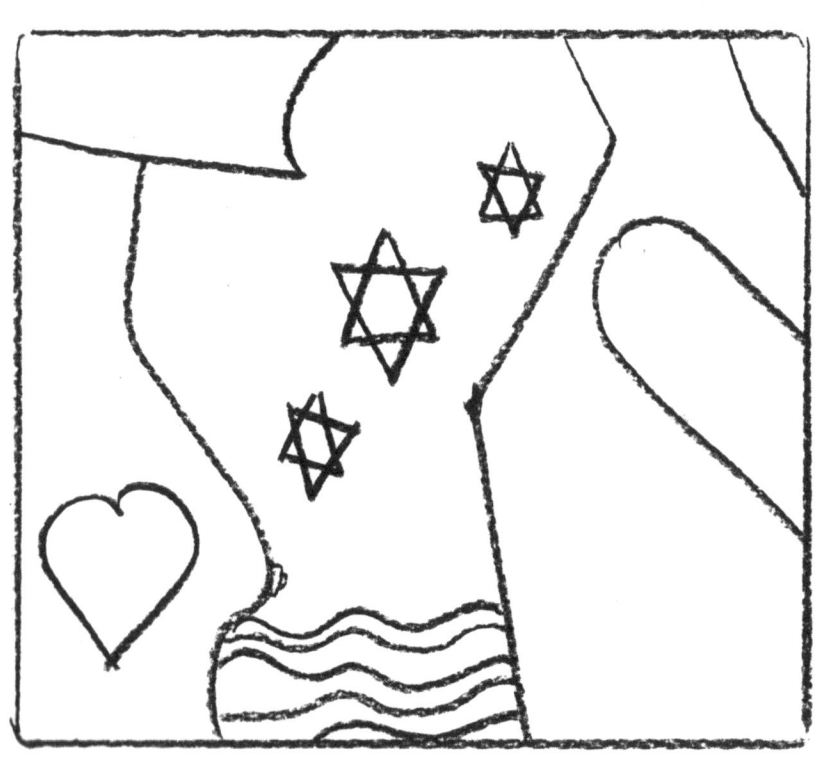

In shadows of the cave we misbehave

Shall we be seen as we seek our delights

Public gardens we have no fears as our bodies

Long to be near

We were not found as we lay on the ground

As I curbed my cries and whispered my sighs

Out at sea you came for me

As my nakedness is before you

I was yours as hands wrapped around

That let me flow completely

A lust and longing a dance of self darkness

All were gifts to me

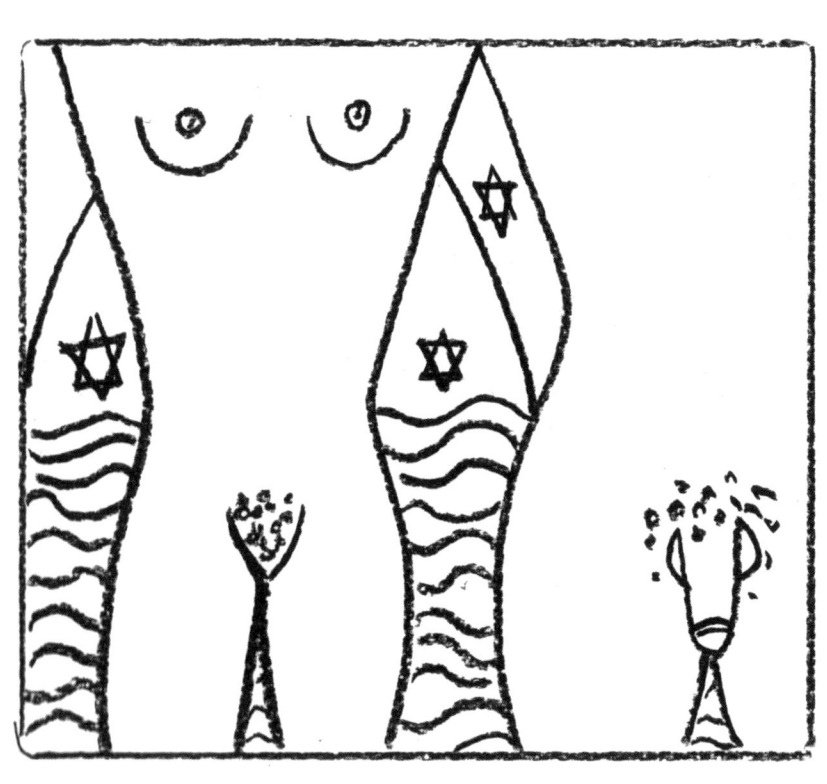

I stood in white not ivory or red

A golden halo above my head

They did not like the look of me so they tore my dress away

The smiling faces disappeared along with the cake

The wine the song

A meadow sweet with romantic views

Was wrenched from my heart too quickly

Sticks and stones death and hate is what they gave to me

Sharp claws vile words

No sweet song of rejoice to be heard

The white dress they hate to see

Such unhappy times with pain all round for me

No white dress no honey moon

As I lay naked on the ground

All saw your wicked ways

And no one said a sound

A man died in front of me

His tears never heard

But in the dark nights do you think of me

Do your deeds go unheard

The white dress no posy of light

Do you have demons in the night

So many souls stood bare and lonely

My family didn't get to play

No wedding no joy but forgiveness on the way

I wandered as a lost mother looking for my child

Over many lands and seas did I travel

To find what I was seeking

A father for my baby

My longing grew like a song

Sweet and tender

Oh so wanting

She awakens this mother for the loss of fair moments

Hugs and kisses

Small hands and feet

They shall not be mine

We did not bear children

I found all this in you

Emptiness I never knew

Longing never fulfilled

I fall into my own heart

And get swallowed by the grief

Soul oh soul

You didn't come with me

A promise made on stars and heaven

Has been forsaken

I struggle to breathe

I can't see tomorrow

Just your face like a shadow

Nothing to hold onto

Nothing to touch

Sound mind have I

As the craziness of grief takes me over

Take me take me she cried

For I have no place to hide

You know the places I will go and so you will follow

I change my name I play the game

It brings us both much pleasure

My hands they are held in strap or bond

The frenzy rises further

A dance a word a position bold

Loud cry of fit or fervour

Take me take me she cries

For no illusion lies

We both like sex

With each other

I am your nightmare

Black and wretched

Twisted like the purple rage

With venom I shall crawl through your dark nights

And wreak havoc on your daily breath

A thousand sharp knives will be sweeter than me

For I will have my day and rob you of your night

No shining star will you see

Nothing to hold onto

You will have no hand of mine

You will die lonely

With the last thought of me

And your betrayal

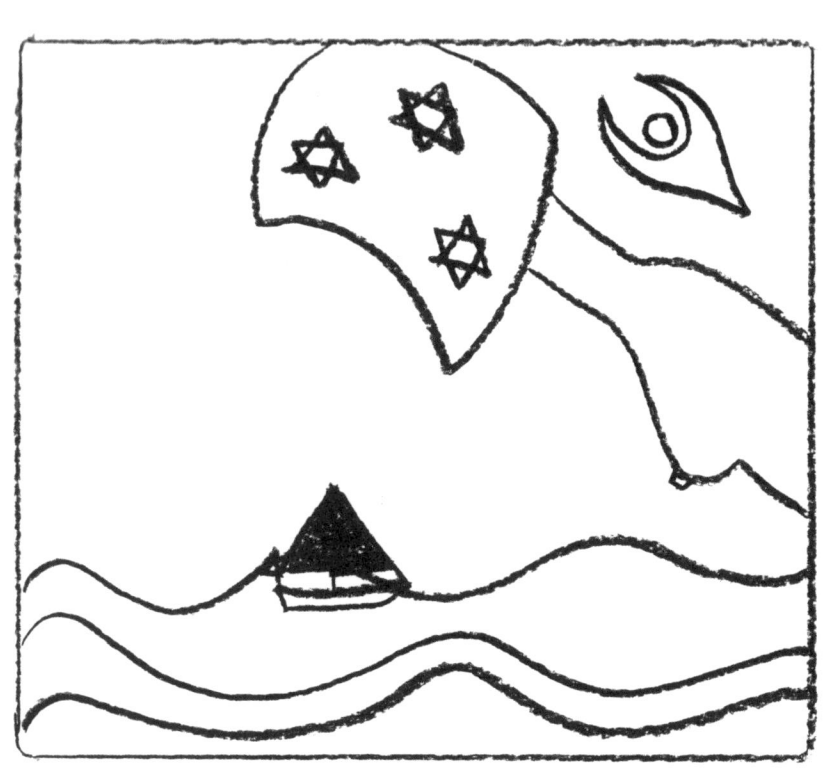

I am this broken woman before you

Was my skin not soft enough and yielding to you

Was not the sea garden a place of delights for you

Was my heart not full enough of love for you

My words my lips my dreams playful desires

Kindness and warmth

Was I not enough for you

I am woman enough for any man

Not you

My tears fall still

A song that was sung

A smile that I saw

Moments that I still cherish

I was shown a world outside of me

I know you saw that too

My tears are for the loss of those dreams

For in my heart I wanted it to be you

Does my pain lessen I think not

We talked of death we talked of life

Of dreams and movements together

Sadness is the only thing that binds us

My place has been taken

Hopes have been stolen

The everlasting love that I had

Has been forsaken

Will you feel the same as me when he holds me tight

And lays me across his bed

Did you not see me this glowing light before you

Has my grace held no interest and wonder

Did my movement in the world not surprise and delight you

The god that lay with me

I saw you watching

Skin to skin mouth to mouth

Have you not watched me and seen me tremble

For I am woman

Mighty and splendid

Have you witnessed my love

Do you not feel it within

I have danced a thousand dances not unseen

It was me who needed to be watching

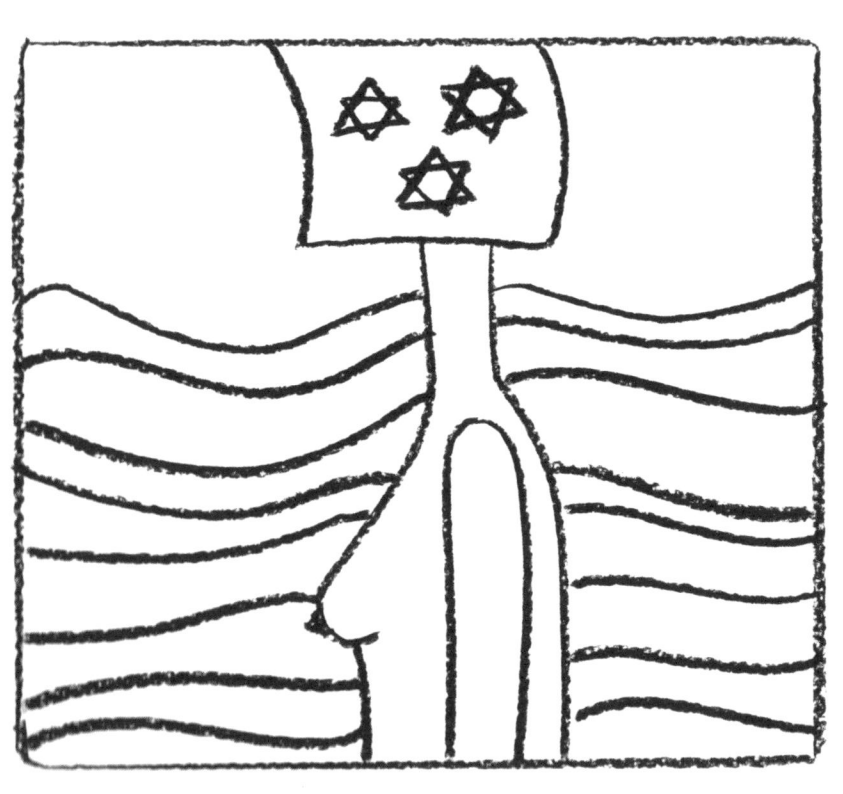

You should watch out on dark nights my love

For I can be found in shadow or light

Plotting my revenge in my strife

A strike at your heart home or lover

See how I wreak havoc in your daily mind

As I have had in mine

Protect your children protect your life

They can't hide from me

I could be god like

But hate rages in me

So watch out do beware

I am a woman

Without a care

No thought for you nothing for me

But the edge of a sharp knife

They did not see I was human

And my soul deeply bled

As they pushed their knives in with smiling faces said

We are so much better than you

For he loves us more

See what we can really do

With sharp fangs and claw

Your brothers mean nothing your father too

Who cares if your mother is dead

For we are much better than you

With gleaming sharp teeth said

Such cutting words

Such cutting deeds

Never seeing how much I bled

You just all sank your teeth in until my dreams were dead

Shame shame on you creatures of the night

Twisted rotten corpses you really are a fright

For no hearts do you have within

Ugliness takes its place

I can't even call you women

Only disgrace

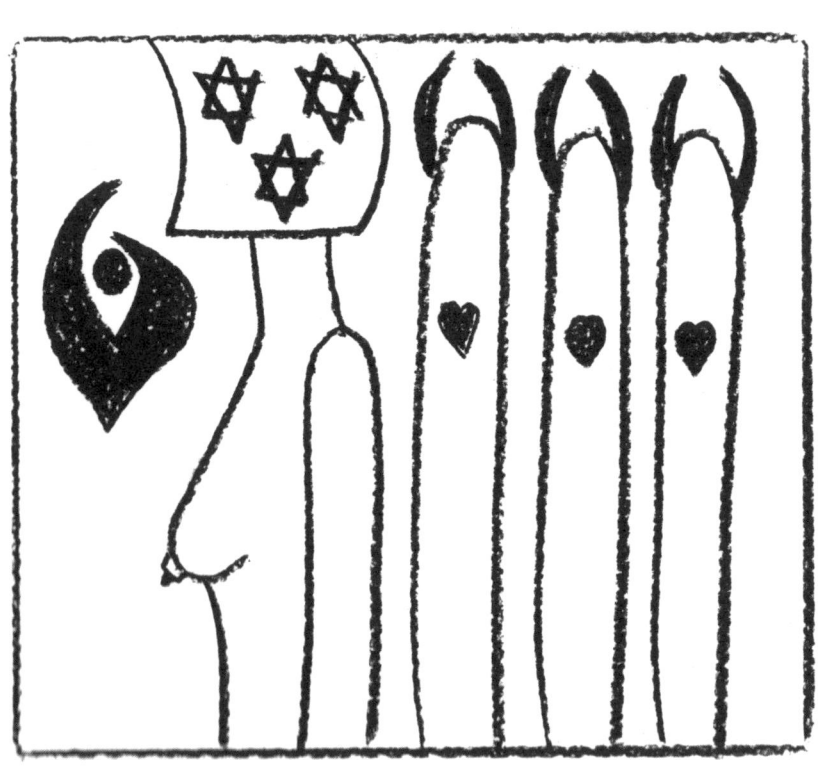

I had love for you all

Did you not see

I would have held you fondly

And oh so preciously

My loving heart would have embraced you tightly

And been strong when you needed me there

I was oh so willing to love you

My words sweet with care

But no you did not see that of me

That I could be a gleam of light

To follow you in your darkness

I can shine oh so bright

My hands I could have given

My love was yours for free

But the saddest thing of all you didn't see this in me

He was so happy with me

Did that not please you as it pleases me

Love and cared for I was there for

No sad loneliness could be found

He was loved he was loved

His heart was broken too

Could you not see

You didn't like to see him happy

Not with me

So unloved hollow inside

Does that please you

Your joy you have not been able to hide

You could have come with me the angel said

There's no place too dark that light can't be shed

I have hands for you to hold onto you see

And light in my eyes that could help you to be free

We could have forever danced

And roamed the ocean blue

You could have come with me

You chose not to

I had already tried on the ring

The wedding dress too

My brother came with me

I wanted to share it with you

His face was full of such joy

As he marched me around the town

Taking me to all the churches

His dreams he had found

Our friends had been invited

Places for joy were made

My mother would have been broken hearted

As the desolation came

No nieces as my bridesmaids

No father by my side

Such pain for my family

My heart still hurts inside

You never even thought of them

Your disgrace you will never hide

I am glad my mother wasn't here

As she would have died

I loved your skin so close to mine

As we lay naked in your bed

Such love I felt for you

But the nightmares said

They screamed at me in the darkest hour

And then I started to dread

No sweet dreams for me

Fear took its place instead

Still you had your nightmares

It was hard to lay in that bed

I hurt when you grabbed me

The anxiety seemed to spread

The nightmares came between us

As all your ghosts played at night

Both of us had nightmares

As we lay naked in the bed

How much I missed your skin

Your hands that held me tight

I couldn't cope with your nightmares

I needed to sleep at night

I loved you so very deeply

And I missed you more and more

My sanity got pushed to its limits

And the bed little I saw

I had to drink to lay with you

And drunk would I come to that place

It was the only way I could cope with them

And all my fears I needed faced

I didn't want to lose you

But you pushed me away at night

I tried to be very loving

And hold you sweet with light

But you blamed me

For the darkness that came to you at night

A woman can only cope with so much

To keep drinking was never right

God how I loved you

As I lay naked in the bed

You could not cope with your nightmares

So you let me go instead

I have not left my room today

As it's so dark inside

I see the sun is shining

But still I sit and hide

I don't want to see you

Or show my pain around

My heart still bleeding

And crying the only sound

I can't leave my room today

And sometimes it feels like I never will

The hardest thing of all is

I love you still

I miss you oh my beloved
And your hand resting on me tight
Songs that have being sung to me
And the love I saw in your eyes
Of warm hot bath waters
And dancing tight
Watching sparkling bright waters
As we glide across them at night
The shining stars above our heads
As we stay out late at sea
Watching old movies
All were the happiest times for me
I miss you my beloved
I wonder do you know
It's hard for me to look at the ocean
The sea garden misses you so

You asked me to forgive you
But you asked nothing of them
I couldn't fight the bitterness
Not now not then
You left her long ago and fell in love with me
But she's the one that holds you
In your place of pain you see
She pours it into your children
Now twisted with scorn
I could fight the bitterness
And our lives having been torn
Broken as we both may be
You let their hatred run
Ripping the heart out of both of us
They think that they have won
What a proud victory
For all the world to see
That's not love my love
Forgiveness will set you free

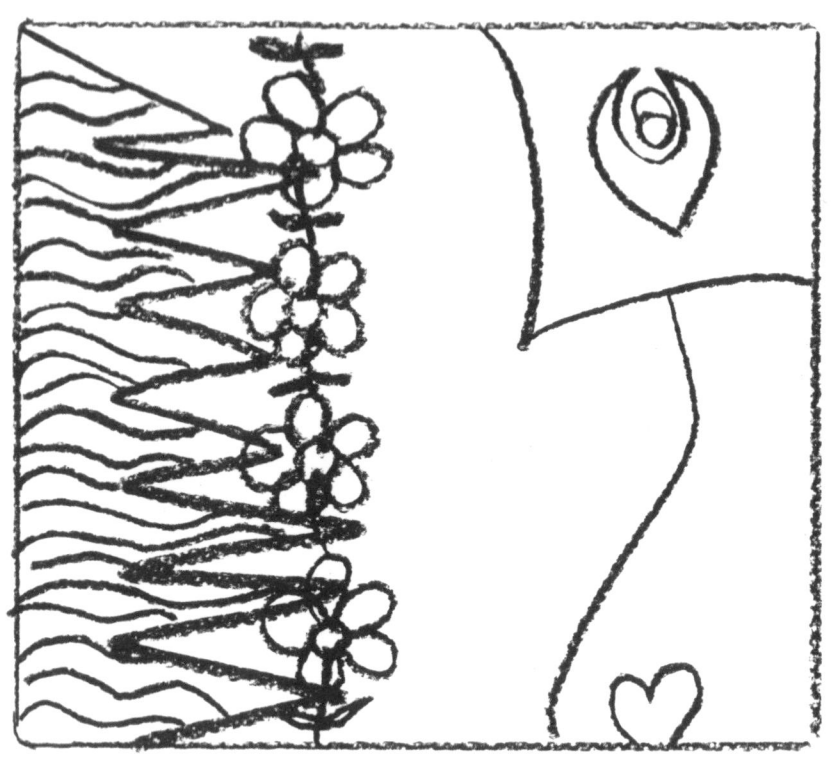

It's coming to the end my love

As I am taken out to sea

Love that was in my heart

But just not meant to be

If so you'd be by my side

And full of joy you would find me

But it's coming to the end my love

As I am taken out to sea

And all my songs and words have been said

I have to let you go

I wonder do you have as much sorrow

I will never know

It's come to the end my love

And I thank you gratefully

For you are the one who got into my heart

I wonder do you miss me

It's at the end my love

And what I need to say

That the gifts that you gave to me

In my heart

Will forever stay

.

SUZANNE CROOK

Photograph by Ruby Ingleheart

'My art has brought me much joy and happiness.

It fulfills a great need in me to be creative, to play and
enjoy the wonders of the world around me.
I appreciate the waves of the sea, laying in
flower-filled meadows and enjoying my being.

Art gives me peace and stillness,
fun, joy and happiness.'

www.theartofhappinessgallery.co.uk